MW01154678

101 Facts About
PREDATORS
101 Facts About

101 FACTS ABOUT

SHARKS

Julia Barnes

Gareth Stevens Publishing
A WORLD ALMANAC EDUCATION GROUP COMPANY

Please visit our web site at: www.garethstevens.com
For a free color catalog describing Gareth Stevens Publishing's
list of high-quality books and multimedia programs,
call 1-800-542-2595 (USA) or 1-800-387-3178 (Canada).
Gareth Stevens Publishing's fax: (414) 332-3567.

Library of Congress Cataloging-in-Publication Data

Barnes, Julia, 1955-
    101 facts about sharks / by Julia Barnes. — North American ed.
      p. cm. — (101 facts about predators)
    Includes bibliographical references and index.
    Summary: Presents information about the physical characteristics, habitat,
and behavior of sharks.
    ISBN 0-8368-4039-9 (lib. bdg.)
    1. Sharks—Miscellanea—Juvenile literature. [1. Sharks—Miscellanea.]
I. Title: One hundred one facts about sharks. II. Title: One hundred and one
facts about sharks. III. Title.
    QL638.9.B348   2004
    597.3—dc22   2003059175

This North American edition first published in 2004 by
Gareth Stevens Publishing
A World Almanac Education Group Company
330 West Olive Street, Suite 100
Milwaukee, WI 53212 USA

This U.S. edition copyright © 2004 by Gareth Stevens, Inc. Original edition © 2003 by First
Stone Publishing. First published in 2003 by First Stone Publishing, 4/5 The Marina,
Harbour Road, Lydney, Gloucestershire, GL15 5ET, United Kingdom. Additional end
matter © 2004 by Gareth Stevens, Inc.

First Stone Series Editor: Claire Horton-Bussey
First Stone Designer: Sarah Williams
Geographical consultant: Miles Ellison
Gareth Stevens Editor: Catherine Gardner

Printed in Hong Kong through Printworks Int. Ltd.

1 2 3 4 5 6 7 8 9 08 07 06 05 04

WHAT IS A PREDATOR?

Predators are nature's hunters, the creatures that must kill in order to survive. They come in all shapes and sizes, ranging from the mighty tiger to a slithering snake.

Although predators are different in many ways, they do have some things in common. All predators are necessary in the balance of nature. Predators keep the number of other animals in control, preventing disease and starvation. In addition, all of them adapted, or changed, to survive where they live. They developed special skills to find **prey** and kill it in the quickest, simplest way possible.

Swimming through the ocean are some of the world's most feared predators. An amazing sense of smell, the abilities to detect invisible vibrations and electrical impulses, and deadly teeth and jaws make sharks exceptional predators.

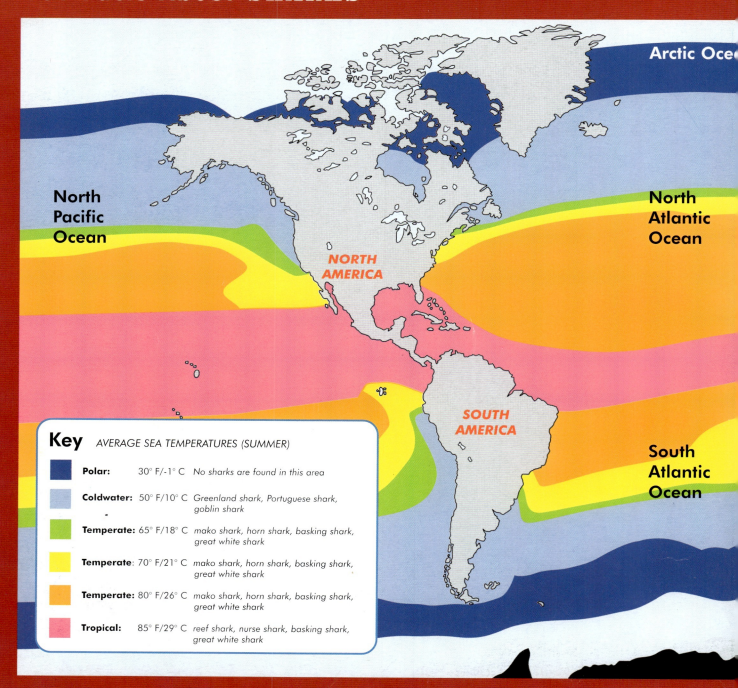

Arctic Ocean

North
Pacific
Ocean

North
Atlantic
Ocean

NORTH
AMERICA

SOUTH
AMERICA

South
Atlantic
Ocean

Key *AVERAGE SEA TEMPERATURES (SUMMER)*

Polar: 30° F/-1° C *No sharks are found in this area*

Coldwater: 50° F/10° C *Greenland shark, Portuguese shark, goblin shark*

Temperate: 65° F/18° C *mako shark, horn shark, basking shark, great white shark*

Temperate: 70° F/21° C *mako shark, horn shark, basking shark, great white shark*

Temperate: 80° F/26° C *mako shark, horn shark, basking shark, great white shark*

Tropical: 85° F/29° C *reef shark, nurse shark, basking shark, great white shark*

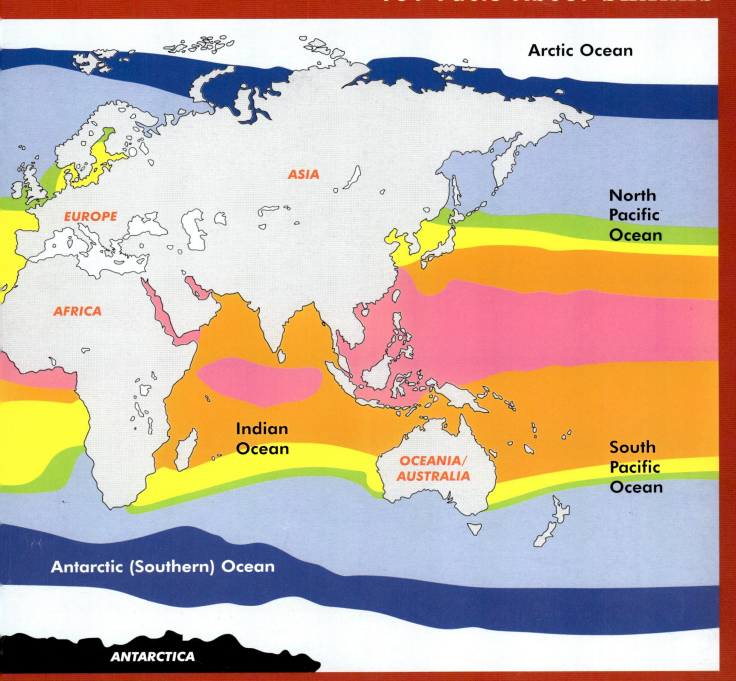

Arctic Ocean

ASIA

North
Pacific
Ocean

EUROPE

AFRICA

South
Pacific
Ocean

Indian
Ocean

OCEANIA/
AUSTRALIA

Antarctic (Southern) Ocean

ANTARCTICA

like small rugs on the bottom of the sea. No matter what their size or their shape, all sharks are types of fish.

1 More than four hundred **species** of sharks live in Earth's oceans. From time to time, scientists find even more kinds of sharks.

2 Sharks grow in many different shapes. Blue sharks have **streamlined**, bullet-shaped bodies, and spotted wobbegongs lie

3 A whale shark (above) is the largest fish in the ocean. Reaching as much as 46 feet (14 meters) long, a whale shark is smaller than the blue whale, a mammal that is 80 feet (24 m) long.

4 The spined pygmy shark grows no longer than 8 inches (20 centimeters).

5 Sharks eat sea animals. Some sharks, such as the great white shark, fiercely hunt big animals, but others, such as the basking shark, swallow huge mouthfuls of tiny **plankton**.

6 Most sharks live and hunt alone most of the time. Others, such as the hammerhead sharks, often swim in groups known as **schools** (right).

7 Nurse sharks and reef sharks are two species found in the warm water of **tropical** climates.

8 The mako, basking, and horn sharks are among the species that prefer water from 50° to 68° Fahrenheit (10° to 20° Celsius). They live in Earth's **temperate** zones.

9 Fewer sharks make their homes in cold water. The sharks that prefer cold water include the Portuguese, frilled (above), and goblin sharks, which swim in some of the deepest parts of the Atlantic and Pacific Oceans.

10 The Greenland shark is the largest species to live in arctic and antarctic waters, including Greenland and South Africa.

11 Most kinds of sharks live in the saltwater of the ocean. Some species, however, visit or even live in the freshwater of rivers and lakes. The bonnethead shark (right) of the western Atlantic and eastern Pacific Oceans, swims to the mouths of rivers to give birth.

12 Bull sharks can live not only in saltwater oceans but also in freshwater rivers and lakes. They swim far inland, in places such as the Amazon River in South America and the Mississippi River in the United States.

13 Scientists think the first kinds of sharks took shape in Earth's oceans about 400 million years ago before many other forms of life existed.

14 Sharks and other fish have the same ancestors, or early relatives. Over time, sharks and fish took on different features.

15 About 100 million years after the first sharks appeared, they entered a golden age. Sharks grew in number and in size. They separated into hundreds of different types.

16 The sharks adapted to survive for millions of years. Their features made them outstanding predators.

17 It looked as though sharks would rule the oceans forever, but about 150 million years ago, many species began to die out.

20 Fossils form as mud covers the bones or teeth of dead animals and slowly turns to rock. Fossils can tell a lot about animals, even those that lived millions of years ago.

18 The best predators survived, and many of their features can be seen in today's sharks (above).

19 Scientists have had trouble finding out about the history of sharks, because shark **fossils** are so hard to find.

21 Shark fossils are rare because sharks are different from other kinds of fish. Most fish have **skeleton** bones that are hard.

22 A shark's skeleton is made of a tough, elastic type of tissue called **cartilage**. Cartilage **decays**

quickly and does not form fossils. Only the teeth of a shark remain over the years.

23 Each kind of shark can be recognized by the shape of its teeth, the number it has, and the way they grow.

24 The shape and pattern of shark teeth have adapted to the way each type hunts and to the kind of prey it eats.

25 The great white shark (right) has two types of teeth. The

shark's upper jaw has larger, triangular teeth that bite through flesh. The lower jaw has long, pointed teeth for holding and slicing its prey.

26 A sand tiger shark has long, thin teeth (below). The size and shape of these teeth help the shark catch and kill the small kinds of fish that share its home in tropical and temperate parts of the ocean.

27 The cookie cutter shark (above right) lives around Australia. It is only 20 inches (50 cm) long, but it eats big prey. It uses its large teeth to cut bite-sized chunks out of the sides of whales and dolphins.

28 The sawfish from the coast of South Australia (below right) uses its saw to stun prey and dig out buried crabs and fish.

29 A shark's main tools for hunting are its teeth. It cannot afford to have dull or missing teeth.

teeth, and it may use thousands in its lifetime.

32 A shark's powerful jaws are attached to its skull by stretchy **muscles** and **tendons**.

30 Behind each row of working teeth are rows of spare teeth that stay folded flat against the gums. When a tooth breaks, a new one moves to a forward and upright position.

33 As a shark attacks its prey, it can thrust its jaws forward. The lower teeth hold the prey while the upper teeth slice it.

31 A shark may have dozens or even hundreds of working

13

34 Depending on their shape and their habitat, sharks use different swimming styles.

35 Some sharks, such as the megamouth, swim slowly. A megamouth, which may be 17 feet (5 m) long, cannot catch speedy prey. It eats plankton and small shrimps that it strains out of the water.

36 For sharks that live on the ocean floor, hunting may be as easy as prowling slowly just above the ground and scooping up any prey they find.

37 Pacific angel sharks just lie in the sand and wait for a meal (above). When they spot fish in reach, they snap up their heads and grab with their huge mouths.

38 For some kinds of sharks, a disguise is the best way to lure prey. A tasselled wobbegong of the western Pacific (below) is the same colors as the rocks and sand. It even has a fringe of tassels that hangs down to look like seaweed.

39 A nurse shark hunts slowly among rocks. It uses its thick lips to suck its prey out of holes and cracks between the rocks.

40 The sharks that need to chase their prey must move fast. They need streamlined, torpedo-shaped bodies to glide easily through the water.

41 Tiny teethlike scales, called denticles, on the shark's skin control the flow of water over its body and help it move faster.

42 The fastest swimmer among sharks is the shortfin mako shark. It can swim at speeds of at least 30 miles (48 kilometers) per hour when it chases fast fish, such as tuna or swordfish.

filled with oil, which is lighter than water. It is so big that it can make up one-quarter of the shark's body weight.

43 Unlike other fish, a shark does not have a swim bladder, the organ that helps fish float.

44 Most sharks are heavier than water. They swim almost all of the time. When they stop, they sink to the ocean floor.

45 A shark has a huge liver, which helps to keep it afloat. The liver is

46 When they swim, sharks use their specially-designed fins to help them move smoothly through the water.

47 The **pectoral fins**, which are the fins on both sides of the body, work like airplane wings (above). As water passes over them, the fins give enough lift to keep the shark from sinking.

48 Like all fish, sharks breathe by taking in water and using their **gills** to remove the oxygen from it.

49 The sharks that have streamlined bodies must swim forward to pump water into their gills. One of the streamlined sharks is the grey reef shark (right), which swims around coral reefs in tropical seas.

50 The sand tiger shark has a different way to get the oxygen it needs. It swims to the surface of the ocean and swallows a huge gulp of air into its stomach. When filled with air, it rests motionless without sinking.

51 To change position, a sand tiger shark just releases some of the air in its stomach. As it swims, its mouth hangs open, an unusual habit for a shark.

54 The blue shark (left) migrates, or moves, amazing distances. The blue sharks that live in the Atlantic Ocean follow the **currents** to cross and recross the ocean in a clockwise pattern.

52 Some sharks have become such good swimmers that they are able to travel long distances.

53 An Atlantic sandbar shark may summer off the northern U.S. coast. It swims south in winter, when it may settle near Florida or in the Gulf of Mexico.

55 The blue sharks that start their journey in the Caribbean Sea go north up the U.S. coast. They cross the Atlantic to reach Europe, head south to western Africa, and return to the Caribbean.

56 Sharks rely on their finely tuned senses to migrate, to stay safe from predators, including other sharks, and to catch prey.

57 Sharks have good eyesight. They can see in color and can make out different shapes.

58 Sharks, such as a swell shark (right), see well in low light. Some sharks hunt at night or in the depths of the ocean.

59 When a shark attacks, its eyes could easily be injured by the teeth, claws, or spines of its victim.

60 To protect its eyes, a shark may have an extra eyelid, known as a nictitating membrane. It slides down over the eye as a shark attacks its prey.

61 Sharks can hear the same sounds that a human can hear. In addition, sharks pick up low-frequency **vibrations** that travel through the water.

shark can smell a tiny odor and follow it a long distance to find food.

62 Vibrations under the water help a shark pick up on changes in ocean currents and locate injured fish that might make a meal.

63 Every animal gives off a little electricity. Sharks can feel the electricity animals give off, and they use this sense to find prey.

64 The most important sense for hunting is a shark's sense of smell. A

65 A hammerhead has one nostril on each side of its head (left). Sharks use nostrils only for smelling. Gills do their breathing.

66 Sharks are adapted to eat the kinds of animals that live in the same places as they do.

67 Many sharks eat any bony fish and squid they find. Other sharks search out certain foods.

68 Hammerheads eat stingrays. Shortfin makos swim fast enough to catch bluefish and swordfish. Great white sharks prey on seals, sea lions, and big fish, such as tuna.

69 Some shark foods may be surprising. Big sharks eat little sharks. Some male sharks eat baby sharks. Lemon sharks eat sea birds that come within reach, along with other fish.

70 All sharks eat other animals. Only some sharks scavenge, or eat the bodies of dead animals, such as whales, they find floating in the water.

71 Hungry tiger sharks (below), which live along tropical coasts, try to eat almost anything they can find — whether it is dead or alive. They even swallow car tires and other garbage.

72 Some fish dare to swim with sharks. Pilot fish and sharksuckers follow sharks closely, ready to grab the scraps that fall as a shark eats its meal.

73 Cleaner fish (below) pick **parasites** off a shark's skin. The cleaner fish often group in certain areas, and sharks visit these areas as needed for service.

74 A remora has a flat sucker on its head. With this sucker, it hangs onto a shark. The remora rides as it hides from danger.

75 Breeding between males and females can get rough. Males follow females, trying for a chance to mate. The males grab at the females with their teeth and may injure them.

76 In some species, the skin of females is three times as thick as that of males. Thick skin protects females from stray bites.

77 Sharks have several ways of giving birth to their young. Females may develop babies inside their bodies, in a way similar to mammals. They give birth to live, fully formed young, which are called pups.

78 Horn sharks, which lurk under ledges, swell sharks, which swim in seaweed, and deep-sea cat sharks (above) are some of the sharks that produce eggs in special cases, which they drop on the ocean floor.

79 The shark develops in the case and lives off the yolk (above). Within twelve months, depending on the species, the shark opens the case to escape.

80 Often, a female shark leaves her egg cases in shallow water, where the pups will be safer. After a storm, empty cases, called mermaid's purses, may wash onto the beach.

81 Tiger sharks, nurse sharks, and mako sharks produce eggs that develop inside the female's body. As an **embryo** grows, it eats the egg yolk and then hatches out.

82 The first shark that hatches eats all of the rest of the eggs and the embryos. Then it is ready to be born as a live pup.

83 The young of the lemon sharks and

hammerhead sharks develop in their mother's **womb**. In the womb, the young stay safe from predators and get the nourishment they need.

84 The pup of a nurse shark (right) stays in the womb for five months before it is born. The frilled shark pup takes two years to develop before it is ready to be born and survive alone.

85 The number of pups a shark can produce varies enormously.

A sand tiger shark produces two pups at a time. A blue shark breeds one hundred pups at once.

86 Female sharks do not feed or care for their young. From the time a shark is born, it must find its food on its own.

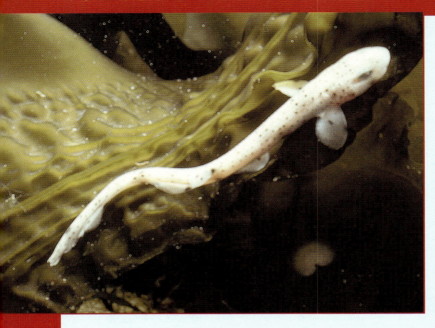

Then they swim to deeper water and larger prey.

89 As the ocean's top predators, sharks of most types have no enemies except humans.

90 Humans kill about 100 million sharks every year for food, for sport, and for products like oil.

87 Female sharks that are ready to give birth may swim to shallower water so their pups can feed on small crabs and shrimps.

88 The lesser spotted dogfish (above) and other pups born near shore grow in the shallow water.

91 Most sharks cannot harm humans. Only a few, such as the tiger shark, bull shark, and great white shark, are responsible for attacks on humans.

92 People are learning more about sharks. Many sharks that were once believed to be great threats to people are not actually so dangerous.

93 If a diver (below), swimmer, or surfer strays too close to some kinds of sharks, the sharks may act in an aggressive way toward the intruder. They may attack a human in self-defense.

94 Some shark attacks happen when the shark mistakes a human for its usual prey.

to be struck by lightning or to drown at the ocean shore than to be killed by a shark.

97 Sharks are not so lucky (left). People use shark teeth for jewelry, shark liver oil for cosmetics, shark skin for leather goods, and shark fins for a favorite soup in some countries.

95 Between sixty and ninety **unprovoked** attacks on people have been reported each year recently. In fewer than fifteen of those attacks, the victim died.

96 Attacks by sharks make newspaper headlines, but they are quite rare. A person is more likely

98 People kill sharks by accident in nets they intended for other fish and on purpose for fun or a big trophy. Some people destroy sharks because they fear such huge predators.

99 Today, the numbers of some types of sharks are declining. A few species are in danger of dying out completely.

100 Sharks need up to fifteen years to grow and begin breeding. Some produce only a few pups at a time. Humans can kill sharks at a faster pace.

101 Although sharks may look scary, we need to understand the part this amazing predator plays in the health of the whole ocean.

 # Glossary

cartilage: tough, elastic tissue that forms a shark's skeleton or a human's ear.

currents: movements of water.

decays: breaks down or rots.

embryo: the developing young of an animal before birth.

fossils: the bones of animals that are preserved in rocks.

gills: organs on either side of the head that help a fish take in oxygen from the water.

muscles: fibers in the body that produce motion.

parasites: creatures that live off of another animal.

pectoral fins: a pair of large fins on either side of a shark's body.

plankton: tiny plants and animals.

predators: animals that kill other animals for food.

prey: an animal a predator chooses to hunt and kill.

schools: groups of fish.

skeleton: the framework of a body, made of bones in humans.

species: types of animals or plants that are alike in many ways.

streamlined: shaped to glide easily.

temperate: having a moderate temperature, neither hot nor cold.

tendons: tissues connecting muscle to other parts of the body.

tropical: having warm, frost-free conditions all year long.

unprovoked: not purposely irritated or forced into action.

vibrations: back-and-forth or quivering movements, such as those made by sound.

womb: part of the female's body where developing young grow.

 # More Books to Read

Shark (Eyewitness series)
Miranda MacQuitty
(DK Publishing)

Sharks (Outside and Inside series)
Sandra Markle
(Atheneum)

**Sharks Keep Losing Their Teeth
(I Didn't Know That series)**
Claire Llewellyn
(Millbrook)

**Great White Sharks
(The Untamed World series)**
Marie Levine
(Raintree/Steck-Vaughn)

 # Web Sites

Florida Museum of Natural History
www.flmnh.ufl.edu/fish/Sharks/
sharks.htm

Sea World
www.seaworld.org/infobooks/
sharks&rays/home.html

KidZone
www.kidzone.ws/sharks/

The Sharksite for Kids
www.sharky-jones.com

To find additional web sites, use a reliable search engine to find one or more of the following keywords: **ocean predator, tiger sharks, shark.**

Index